DONALD TRUMP

An Unbiased View on Everything You Need to Know About Your 45th President

BY

K. CONNORS

© Copyright 2017 By K. Connors - All Rights Reserved.

Copyright © 2017 *Donald Trump.* All rights reserved. No part of this publication may be reproduced, distributed, or transmitted in any form or by any means, including photocopying, recording, or other electronic or mechanical methods, without the prior written permission of the publisher, except in the case of brief quotations embodied in critical reviews and certain other noncommercial uses permitted by copyright law. This also includes conveying via e-mail without permission in writing from the publisher. All information within this book is of relevant content and written solely for motivation and direction. No financial guarantees. All information is considered valid and factual to the writer's knowledge. The author is not associated or affiliated with any company or brand mentioned in the book, therefore does not purposefully advertise nor receives payment for doing so.

Table of Contents

CHAPTER 1: DONALD TRUMP'S HISTORY 1

CHAPTER 2L: THE TRUMP FAMILY 6

CHAPTER 3: ACCOMPLISHMENTS AND DEALS 7

CHAPTER 4: TIES WITH INTERNATIONAL COUNTRIES 9

CHAPTER 5: DONALD TRUMP'S WEALTH 10

CHAPTER 6: HOW HE BEAT THE IRS 14

CHAPTER 7: NOTABLE CHARITIES AND UNIVERSITIES 17

CHAPTER 8: THE KEY FACTORS IN WINNING THE PRESIDENCY 19

CHAPTER 9: HIS NON-POLITICALLY CORRECT APPROACH 23

CHAPTER 10: PRESIDENTIAL POLICIES 25

CHAPTER 11: WHAT TO EXPECT IN THE NEXT FOUR YEARS SHOULD TRUMP'S POLITICAL RIVALS BE CORRECT 27

CHAPTER 12: MAJOR DIFFERENCES BETWEEN THE REPUBLICANS AND DEMOCRATS 31

CHAPTER 1
DONALD TRUMP'S HISTORY

Donald J Trump was born to parents Fred Christ Trump and Mary Anne MacLeod on June 14, 1946. His father, Fred Trump was a prominent American builder and real estate developer. Donald was educated at New York Military Academy from the age of thirteen after a troubled time at the Kew-Forest School in Forest Hills, Queens. At NYMA he earned academic honors and excelled in basketball, soccer, and football. In 1968 he went on to graduate from the Wharton School of the University of Pennsylvania with a bachelor of science in economics and concentration in finance. After his graduation, he joined his father in his business venture.

Thus, his career began with the Trump Organization. His first project was on the revitalization of the Swifton Village apartment complex in Ohio. They cleared it with $6 million profit when they sold it for $12 million. He worked jointly with his father for five years, and then later moved to Manhattan, where he saw success in real estate again. He is presently the Chairman and CEO of the Trump Organization. He is also the founder of Trump Entertainment Resorts which has numerous casinos and hotels around the world.

The brand name Trump is synonymous with prestigious of addresses. Trump International Hotel & Tower which opened in 1997, a 52-storied luxury hotel and residential building, received double Mobil Five-Star ratings for both the hotel and its restaurant, Jean- Georges. It remains to be one of the only three properties in the country to be awarded this rating.

Donald Trump is also a world-class golf course developer. He has many award winning courses in New York, New Jersey, Los Angeles, Palm Beach and much more which are estimated to be valued at $127 million.

In the after effects of the recession in 1989, he was unable to repay loans and had to face the financial turbulence from 1989 to 1997. However, he managed to emerge from the bankruptcy completely in 2005. His company re-emerged as Trump Entertainment Resorts Holdings. Although, as with many others, he had to face financial crisis once again in 2008.

Apart from being a prominent business magnate, he is also a television personality and author. He had appeared in many television series and films, appearing as a caricatured version of himself. Later in 2003, he also became the executive producer of and hosted the reality show "The Apprentice." He also owns the Miss Universe Organization that produces the Miss Universe, Miss USA, and Miss Teen USA pageants. With his success in real estate and television, he further diversified his signature among various fields that include Trump Financial, Trump University, and Donald J. Trump Signature Collection to name a few.

What we are seeing today is that the bravado of Donald Trump along with his vast arsenal of wealth has captivated the media, which has catapulted him as the leading Republican contender to succeed President Obama. The landscape of politics today has forever changed. Ever since 9/11, we have entered into a far darker, more cynical era. The age of serenity we had during the 1950's and 60's has been wiped out by the terrorist attacks of the World Trade center. As a consequence, political campaigns have become more intrusive, more disingenuous and more virulent. No longer are the proper protocols of the past the norm. The etiquette of political campaigns where issues dominate have now been cast aside. We have allowed political candidates to embattle each other instead of offering a unity of purpose with a plan of direction for our nation's future. As a result, many believe that we really have succumbed to a new low in our democratic process as a result.

Trump's rise, in the polls and early primary victories, probably isn't a surprise considering the amount of frustration many Americans have been feeling lately. Also, when we look back in history, there really are similarities between Donald Trump and past leaders of nations. First, we take a look at Julius Caesar, the Roman populist, and demagogue. Today, Trump's appealing qualities resounding with a segment of the population that is both frustrated and angered at the current political atmosphere very much like in Julius Caesars time. This is where both appealed to the resentments of the downtrodden. Whether or not Trump is seeking to solidify power while Caesar sought to make a dictatorship backed by the popular will remains to be seen. Nevertheless, clearly Donald Trump was able to ignite just enough fury of the American populace to win the general election. Looking back, in ancient Rome, it was Caesar, whose lofty ambition and by popular demand, changed the political landscape of Rome forever. Before the rise of Caesar, Rome was a democratic society, but, when Caesar came back from his conquest of Egypt backed by widespread support, he solidified his power and became virtually a dictator.

The irony is that the established political system of the day realized Caesar was a threat to the established order that had been in place for over 500 years. Soon, the political leadership in realizing Caesar posed a real fundamental challenge to the ruling class turned against him. Caesar, eventually, was taken down, in the most brutal of manners, on the Ides of March. In the aftermath, the whole political structure of Rome was changed. The democratic structure that had been the norm soon became obsolete. Democracy was replaced by dictatorships and the fall of Rome had begun.

In the election, we found that Donald Trump used a divided country to his distinct advantage. In reality, though many Americans think that Trump is unacceptable as a presidential candidate, there is also the other side of the coin whom think he is the perfect candidate. Respectfully, there are valid points to both sides. So, why is Donald Trump so successful at attracting such media attention and forming a coalition of voters that have carried him to that lofty position as the President of the United States? He has done so because we as a nation have been split by strong partisan ideologies. Any one of the respective party candidates could have done the exact same thing, and while many tried, Donald Trump did it best.

Now, let's wind back to the 20th century at a time where Hitler rose to power on a nationalist message. A message that transcended throughout Germany following World War I's harsh realization that Germany had to bear. The war reparations that Germany had to face put the German nation virtually in poverty. The consequences of such harsh realities of the early 1920's following the War made the political climate ripe for someone like Hitler to invoke a new nationalism sparking hope and a resurgence of the economic might of the German people. To some, this sounds quite familiar to the most recent Trump campaign. The one thing that Hitler did that was so successful was unifying the many political ideologies into one unified national movement beguiling the public all along the way. However, the way that Hitler came to power isn't what made him an evil man; it is what he did with that power that left a deep scar in our world. To say that Trump will follow in those footsteps is ignorant to say the least, whatever your political affiliation.

It is time for the American public to realize just what exactly is happening to the Democratic process that has been the cornerstone of our Nation for over 240 years. Questions that I hear often are: Are we susceptible to the same fate as Rome? A period where apathy played a very internal role in the demise of Rome's democratic process. Are we as a nation now so enthralled with a political candidate who is demonstrating a keen knack to attract a disenfranchised public into believing that he and he alone will resurrect the American mighty we had following World War II? And, in doing so allowing history to again repeat.

On the other hand, he is not afraid to speak his mind. Many individuals want a President that gets right to the point, doesn't beat around the bush, and tells it like it is. Trump is a fresh face that much of America was looking for. His entire campaign, as rickety as it may have been, revolved around him wanting to make an actual difference in America. He wasn't your average politician trying to say whatever it was he or she thought people wanted to hear. Regardless of what many think, his immigration policy is actually sound (More on this in another book). Despite what the media choses to cover and not cover, Trump is squeaky clean. Being a public figure for as long as he has, despite one nasty divorce (which is all to common nowadays), we find no encounters with the law, personal issues or outrageous threats of violence. The same can obviously not be said about some of his presidential rivals.

We need to acknowledge that the United States is a nation of diversity, but with that diversity, we have always been a united nation despite the many ethnic groups, religion, and cultures that make our country unique. Even with our diversity, we have always been able to put aside our differences and unite behind a plan of direction for our nation to rise above adversity and solidify the future for generations to come.

CHAPTER 2
THE TRUMP FAMILY

Donald Trump has been married three times and has five children, plus eight grandchildren. Trump, who was raised in Queens, came from a big family before starting one of his own; he's one of five children himself.

DONALD TRUMP'S PARENTS

Donald Trump was born in Queens in 1946 to Fred and Mary Trump. Fred was a Bronx-born New Yorker who made a fortune constructing middle-income apartments in Brooklyn and Queens. Mary was a Scottish immigrant. Donald Trump is the fourth of five children. His sister, Elizabeth, is a former Chase banker; his other sister, Maryanne, is a retired judge who served on the U.S. Court of Appeals for the Third Circuit; his brother, Robert, served as a top Trump executive. However, the sibling who has perhaps garnered the most media attention is Freddy, who died of alcoholism in 1981 at the age of 43; whom Trump often references when discussing his decision to abstain from alcohol his entire life.

CHAPTER 3

ACCOMPLISHMENTS AND DEALS

Donald is the Chairman and CEO of the Trump Organization, a US-based real-estate developing company. He is also the founder of Trump Entertainment Resorts, which holds a large number of casinos and hotels all over the world. He became a celebrity for years due to his extravagant lifestyle and outspoken manner and of course his well-watched successful NBC reality TV show, The Apprentice on which he worked as a host and at the same time executive producer.

He is the fourth child among five children of Fred Trump, a very successful real estate developer based in New York City. It was Donald's father who made a strong influence on his goals to achieve and make a name for himself in real estate development. After obtaining a degree at the Wharton School at the University of Pennsylvania in 1968, he joined his father's company, the Trump Organization.

His first step to his real estate world started when he headed the renovation of the Commodore Hotel into the Grand Hyatt with the Pritzker family. Next was the Trump Tower in New York City along with other residential projects. On other businesses, he expanded his airline industry through purchasing the Eastern Shuttle routes. He also handles his Atlantic City casino business which includes buying the Taj Mahal Casino from the Crosby family. This expansion resulted in mounting debt at the time. Some say this was one of many terrible business decision that he made, while others say that it was simply an experiment that failed. After all, most successful businessmen have made mistakes along the way, only to learn from them and become more successful afterwards.

Back in 2001, he completed Trump World Tower, a 72-story residential tower across from the United Nations Headquarters. He also began the construction of Trump Place, a multi-building development along the Hudson River. He also owns commercial space in Trump International Hotel and Tower, a 44-story mixed-use (hotel and condominium) tower on Columbus Circle. At present, he owns several million square feet of prime Manhattan real estate and remains a major figure in the field of real estate in the United States and a celebrity for his prominent media exposure.

CHAPTER 4

TIES WITH INTERNATIONAL COUNTRIES

Trump's foreign business with 144 companies in 25 countries

In his most recent financial disclosures, Trump listed 144 individual companies that have had dealings in at least 25 countries in Asia, Europe, Africa, South America and North America, among other companies with regional international interests, according to a CNN review. Those business interests have ranged from beverage sales in Israel to golf course developments in the UAE. Although the location of some of Trump's foreign business deals could overlap with future foreign policy decisions, many of Trump's foreign business ties involve licensing deals, in which another party owns the property and pays Trump to use his brand. The Trump Organization has created multiple companies to individually handle each of these deals.

Some of Trump's dealings have already become a focal point of controversy, such as Trump Towers Istanbul, which received criticism from Turkish President Recep Tayyip Erdogan after Trump proposed a ban on Muslims entering the U.S. Despite the revelations from the lengthy disclosures Trump filed during his presidential campaign, the full extent of his international business ties remain relatively unknown.

CHAPTER 5

DONALD TRUMP'S WEALTH

Donald Trump can be easily counted as one of the most recognizable personalities in the world. He is an American business tycoon, a television personality, socialite, and author who has managed to make his presence felt all over the world.

He owns the much popular Trump Entertainment Resorts, which runs casinos and hotels in places all over the world. The Trump Taj Mahal, Trump Plaza, and Trump Marina are all branded Trump casinos. The majority of his investments are in real estate, and he also lends his name to other ventures as a part of their promotion.

He has his very own star on the Hollywood walk of fame for his much-acclaimed television show, "The Apprentice." At 2007, the Forbes estimated Trump's total wealth to be around three billion dollars. In addition to real estate, Trump has also invested in other fields like wrestling and golf courses. He also is a two-time Emmy Award-nominated personality for his roles in movies. He even owns the rights to the Miss Universe organization and as mentioned before, produces Miss Universe, Miss USA, and Miss Teen USA.

His "Trump International Hotel and Tower" projects have been completed in the most happening cities of Chicago and Las Vegas and are one of the most profitable ventures thus far, with many more ventures still under construction. He has also authored several books on management and real estate. Thus, Donald Trump, with his diverse interests and commanding personality has been, is, and will remain one of the most watched and successful celebrities in the world.

An Asset Breakdown of Donald Trump's Wealth

1. Trump Tower (New York City)

Trump Owns: 244,000 sq. ft.

Total Value: $471 million

Net Value: $371 million

2. 1290 Avenue of the Americas (New York City)

Trump Owns: 30%

Total Value: $2.31 billion

Net Value: $409 million

3. Niketown (New York City)

Trump Owns: Ground lease through 2079

Total Value: $400 million

Net Value: $390 million

4. 40 Wall Street (New York City)

Trump Owns: Ground lease through 2059

Total Value: $501 million

Net Value: $345 million

5. Trump Park Avenue (New York City)

Trump Owns: 49,564 sq. ft. of condos; 27,467 sq. ft. of retail

Total Value: $191 million

Net Value: $177 million

6. Trump Parc/Trump Parc East (New York City)

Trump Owns: 11,750 sq. ft. of condos; 14,963 sq. feet of retail; 13,108 sq. ft. of garage

Total Value: $88 million

Net Value: $88 million

7. Trump International Hotel and Tower, Central Park West (New York City)

Trump Owns 10,578 sq. ft. of retail; 18,370 sq. ft. of garage; one 460-sq.-ft. Condo

Total Value: $38 million

Net Value: $38 million

8. Trump World Tower, 845 United Nations Plaza (New York City)

Trump Owns 9,007 sq. ft. of retail; 28,579 sq. ft. of garage; one 2,835-square-foot condo

Total Value: $27 million

Net Value: $27 million

9. Spring Creek Towers (Brooklyn, N.Y.)

Trump Owns: 4% stake

Total Value: $1 billion

Net value: $25 million

10. **Trump Plaza (New York City)**

    Trump Owns: Ground lease through 2082

    Total Value: $27.7 million

    Net Value: $13 million

11. **Trump Tower Penthouse (New York City)**

    Trump Owns: 30,000 sq. ft.

    Total Value: $90 million

    Net Value: $90 million

12. **555 California Street (San Francisco)**

    Trump Owns: 30% stake

    Value: $1.645 billion

    Net Value: $317 million

CHAPTER 6

HOW HE BEAT THE IRS

Please note that this material has been prepared for informational purposes only, and is not intended to provide, and should not be relied on for, tax, legal or accounting advice. You should consult your own tax, legal and accounting advisors before engaging in any transaction

As many of you know, "The Donald" invests heavily in real estate. One of the biggest deductions for real estate investors is depreciation. The way they maximize the deduction for depreciation is to:

1. Increase the depreciable basis of the asset; take the higher of either the tax roll or an independent appraiser's evaluation.

2. Decrease the length of time the asset is depreciated, identify personal property assets. They can be depreciated over shorter lives.

Mr. Trump most likely has not paid taxes throughout the years by using a tax strategy known as the "Tax Deferred Exchange." This is a fantastic way to take all of one's profits from a sale of real estate and put it into a new property without having initially to pay taxes. When his property is transferred at death, the basis is adjusted to current market values, thus all or mostly all of the deferred capital gains tax liabilities can be eliminated.

How do others accomplish the same thing?

1. Funds from the sale are held by a qualified intermediary or an accommodator until the exchange transaction is complete, with the requirements having been met.

2. The individual has 45 days from the date escrow closes to identify an "up property" and 180 days to complete the exchange. The 180 days includes the 45-day identification period.

3. If the individual receives cash or reduction in the mortgages, it's considered "boot" and they will have to pay capital gains taxes on it.

One of the advantages of doing a tax-free exchange is that you retain more of the funds for investment and defer taxes to a later date. Postponing the taxes is a good tax strategy because, when the taxes are finally paid, they're generally paid with inflationary dollars. The longer the payment is delayed, the lower the present value of the taxes and the larger the benefit of the deferment.

Donald Trump is proposing four tax brackets topping out at 25% No tax on individuals earning less than $25,000, couples earning less than $50,000. He also intends to replace the corporate rate with a maximum 15% tax, as well as end tax breaks for business earnings overseas. Note how he would not eliminate the two primary strategies for real estate investors.

To add a little debate into the mix, Hillary Clinton wanted to increase the capital gains rate. Bernie Sanders wanted to tax capital gains and dividends taxed at the same rates as incomes for annual incomes over $250,000 at 52%. Ted Cruz wanted a flat tax of 10% on capital gains and to abolish the Internal Revenue Service. Marco Rubio wanted to eliminate capital gains taxes altogether.

Trump's tax returns will show us many new strategies to reduce income taxes using real estate. The return, if it's forthcoming, will make interesting reading. It will point out the difference between taxable and nontaxable profits. You may even be able to verify his billionaire status and determine if he is a huge taxpayer, or uses legitimate rules to avoid huge levies.

CHAPTER 7

NOTABLE CHARITIES AND UNIVERSITIES

DONALD TRUMP UNIVERSITIES

Fortunately, Donald Trump had made it easier for those aspiring to the secrets of wealth. He has given us Trump University and in particular, the Wealth Builders Blueprint. Trump University is an online university, offering correspondence courses in real estate, entrepreneurship, management negotiation and wealth creation. It boasts 100,000 students in over 100 countries worldwide and has brought education pioneers together and compiled a curriculum which has been packaged as online courses, CD audio courses, discussion groups and email newsletters, as well as speaking dates for Donald Trump and his associates.

Whether you want to learn about debt elimination, personal finance, real estate investing, evaluating stocks, trading options, or just simply how to start your own business and build a fortune, Trump University provides courses which cover all of the above. They also offer telephone coaching.

The Trump University's signature program is the Wealth Builders Blueprint. It is a comprehensive, seven hour home study course that claims success is virtually guaranteed if you follow the program. The Wealth Builders Blueprint covers issues such as... turning goals into action, mastering the mysteries of money, how to persuade others to pay for your talents and ideas, starting a business, retiring on real estate riches, how to excel in your career.

The course claims to provide 60 detailed action steps, precisely calculated to deliver real-world results. No one else can be Donald Trump because he's the only one that looks out at the world through those eyes. However, Trump University offers to teach the same secrets he used to achieve the kind of outstanding success that has elevated him to guru status among business hopefuls.

DONALD TRUMP'S CHARITIES

Trump describes himself as an "ardent philanthropist" whose charitable activities are "an integral part of his ethos. He is the archetypal businessman and an icon of New York." Oh, he is also "the most recognized businessman in the world," a trailblazer whose "acumen is unrivaled, and the diversity of his interests has set a new paradigm in the world of business."

Donations from the billionaire's foundation appear to be mere crumbs falling from his overflowing plate. In 2009, the group–flush with WWE cash–gave $26,000 to the American Cancer Society, $5000 to the Alzheimer's Association, $6000 to the Make-A-Wish Foundation, and $250 for the Special Olympics. Trump, an avid golfer, also donated $100,000 apiece to the Tiger Woods Foundation, the William J. Clinton Foundation, and a hospital foundation connected to Arnold Palmer. Trump also donated $75,000 to the foundation of golfer Annika Sorenstam, $5000 to Golf Pros Beating Cancer, and $1000 to the Metropolitan Golf Association Foundation.

Trump has also been a regular contributor to the foundations of New York Yankee Derek Jeter and ex-Bronx Bombers manager Joe Torre, as well as the New York Jets Foundation. While he has donated $25,000 to the Ronald Reagan Presidential Foundation, Trump also wrote a $5000 check to the Edward M. Kennedy Center for Study of the United States.

The recipient of the largest single Trump donations has been the United Way of New York City, which received $250,000 in 2004 and 2006. The Police Athletic League has also received large donations from Trump, who sits on the group's board of directors.

CHAPTER 8

THE KEY FACTORS IN WINNING THE PRESIDENCY

To be president of the United States of America you should have certain character traits that include conflict resolution, being a visionary, diplomacy, a sound worldview perspective, and a love for humanity.

If we go back to presidential cycles prior to 2008 and ask the question, could a person like Donald Trump be elected president? The answer would more than likely be a resounding "No" because the political climate then was not influenced by that of what it is today. However, with the twists and turns our economy and foreign rivals have undergone, many would argue that Donald Trump is the ideal President for the state that our country is in.

Donald Trump is not the first wealthy man that has ventured into the political arena to contest the presidential election and win a seat at the podium. This list includes Ross Perot (independent, 1992), Steve Forbes (Republican, 1996 and 2000), John Kerry (Democrat, 1996 and 2000), and Mitt Romney (Republican, 2012).

The problem many voters have with wealthy political candidates is that they cannot always be trusted. Presumably, because they are privileged and do not always fully understand the challenges that working-class people are faced with. With the exception of Kerry and Romney, these wealthy presidential candidates also lacked political experience.

There are good reasons why a political neophyte like Donald Trump was the front-runner over his more experienced political opponents. This field of Republican presidential candidates was, respectfully, a weak one that included individuals who have had for the most part no significant political accomplishments or leadership qualities. This combined with the majority of America wanting a change in leadership styles, along with the many years of stagnant democratic presidencies, provided an ideal spotlight for Donald Trump to stand in.

What they had was a penchant for tough talk, which usually involved bashing eachother (more commonly known in politics as mud slinging) or doing controversial things like signing a letter to Iran's Ayatollah, shutting down the government, and their mantra of repealing Obamacare.

Another example as to what made it so easy for Donald Trump to win the Presidency was the incompetence of the Democratic Party. First, Clinton, being the nominee for the party offered no palpable change. She wanted to continue down the road President Obama began on eight years ago. Many Americans grew tired of this stagnant state of nothing and wanted a real change, not someone who was going to keep us on the same path for at least another four years. Trump, represented a change. Whether it's a good change or a bad one, it is a change nonetheless. Secondly, the Democratic Party showed the world that they have completely lost the art of negotiating. Instead of properly campaigning for votes in swing states, the Clinton campaign was more focused on celebrity endorsements. Then afterwards, were appalled that the political acumen of Cher and Beyonce counted for almost nothing. Shocker there!

The left may have won the cultural war, but they certainly couldn't find a common ground with the majority of the voter population. It's no secret that almost every single poll was wrong about the outcome of the election. This is because many people are too scared to speak their mind when questioned, mainly because it has become a social standard not accept the beliefs or ideas of anybody else. There is no discussion anymore... No more critical thinking; just insults and labels being thrown about freely.

However, when in the voting booth all alone, with no judgments, nobody watching, nobody to question your beliefs or opinions, this becomes a very powerful thing. The Trump campaign hit the nail on the head when they said they would win the silent majority. Looks like they were right.

Below are two very important ways the Trump Campaign used the emotions of the American people to their advantage.

1. TV celebrity status - Donald Trump's egotistical personality has been enlarged not because of his wealth, but because of his TV reality show - The Apprentice. The show has made him a TV celebrity, and boy do we love our celebrities. Donald Trump's celebrity TV status has given him the insight on how to act and talk to the TV media – Not always to help his numbers, but to get a *reaction*. Reactions mean coverage, and coverage means he has more air-time than any other candidate out there. This experience along with his outspoken style make it appear that he is beholden to no one. If he is beholden to anyone, it is his egotistical alter ego – Many thought that this would be his ultimate downfall in the Presidential Election. I guess just over 65 million people were wrong about this.

2. The politics of illusion – These days, everything in politics seems to be an illusion of horrors. This illusion had always been around, but started to gain more traction in 2008 when the GOP had begun their crusade to make President Obama an unpopular president. During the campaign for his second term, the crusade picked up momentum with things like voter suppression, the several "scandal" hearings against his administration, and endless propaganda aimed at demonizing and delegitimizing him. The net result of the GOP's anti-Obama crusade is that the illusion was created that President Obama was the worst President and was taking the country down the wrong path. This illusion has caused disenchantment among

conservative voters and probably those that are still on the fence.

The disenchantment is similar to what Americans felt in 2008 and that played a part in electing President Obama as the first African-American president. Despite what some think of Donald Trump, this disenchantment helped him get elected as the first wealthy businessman without years of political experience.

CHAPTER 9

HIS NON-POLITICALLY CORRECT APPROACH

Some of the Trump non-political approach includes:

1. GUTSY ATTITUDE

While President Obama was successful in his stint in bringing the recession under control, taking out Osama Bin Laden, and bringing back many troops from Iraq, he did not deliver on many of his poll promises of ushering in large-scale reforms. His attempts to keep everyone happy have backfired on his policies. Trump, on the other hand, has proven that he is not hesitant to speak his mind, even if it puts him in hot water. The world may just need a gutsy leader like this to deal with these types of mounting problems.

2. CONFIDENCE

The huge majority of electoral votes that Trump won with shows that the people of America are willing to trust him. This and his lack of "politically correct" conversational pieces show that he has the confidence to indirectly, or directly say "I don't care what you think, I'll get it done without you". Many leaders aspire to this level of confidence, while it is important to keep in check to what extent you take it.

3. WILLINGNESS TO LEARN

His change in attitude towards Obama, admitting there are some good migrants and willingness to keep some areas off limits with the wall between the U.S. and Mexico show that he is willing to learn and adapt to changing circumstances.

4. OUTSIDER APPROACHES

Trump is not from the political establishment, and the construction magnate is the 'outsider' who is concerned about the economic downturn, ISIS attacks, migrant crisis, rising unemployment, stagnant jobs and wages, violent domestic attacks and many other issues that are plaguing the U.S. He is not hesitant to admit the problems, and like the proverbial outsider is interested in fixing those problems. This outsider approach will prove very beneficial when discussing policies passed by striking a proper tone with the Senate and House leadership.

Above all, there is his strong business acumen to guide him in doing what is best for the country. Afterall, maybe running the country like a business is what America needs in order to kick start the nation back to where we used to be?

5. STRONG POLITICAL INSTINCTS

The political instincts he has, or at least that of what he thinks he has, are strong and inarguable. When Trump and his advisors argued that the "silent voters" will back him, few actually believed his words. Yet, he had the last laugh on the morning of November 9. It is expected that these instincts will help him to take the right path during his Presidency.

CHAPTER 10
PRESIDENTIAL POLICIES

Depending of course on what side of the American political spectrum from which they are speaking, people love to comment on and critique Trump's proposed policies. If not the voting American, then many others have no fear in weighing in on the controversial conversation themselves. The mannerly in us can put this down to his celebrity image, his commercial successes, and ultimately the unyielding relationship between his fame and his fortune.

However, there is of course, another us; a very large cross section of a community that might find his no nonsense, no hands on the handlebar, flip-flopping, blunt speaking and atypical approach to politics more than just an electoral stunt. He is seen to be giving a nation a voice; some even say abetting a populist revolt.

It is a little difficult, however, to understand why so many political pundits are baffled over his ability to break all the political rules. Sure, much of Trump's one-liners may "offend" some guarded sensibilities; his off-color condemnation of undocumented Mexican migrants and calls to build a wall on the US-Mexican border and temporarily prevent all Muslims from entering the US, for example, might be confronting. However, just because an individual says something that may be "offensive", does not constitute ill wishing upon that person. What is offensive to one, may or may not be offensive to another. There is no law against offensive remarks, as it is all subjective to the individual as a person. It is important to make decisions based on facts, as emotional, uninformed, fallacious reasoning may lead to unpleasant outcomes.

Yet, once we peel away the political rhetoric, the noise, the campaign strategist's use of predictive analytics, there are factors in Trump's campaign that run parallel to what is an emergent and growing swell in Australia - political correctness and the public's unconscious fall for Freud's theory of psychological projection.

Freud considered that in projection thoughts, motivations, desires, and feelings that cannot be accepted as one's own are dealt with by being placed in the outside world and attributed to someone else. Of course, nothing is easy when it comes to Freudian psychoanalysis - he went on to talk about how what the ego repudiates is split off and placed in another. So, basically, this is blame shifting. We defend ourselves against our own unpleasant impulses by denying their existence while attributing them to others.

Americans, having grown tired of the political correctness mantra, having been told what they must accept, what they can and can't say are, as are Australians, projecting their inner (perhaps true) feelings and thoughts on that man who even his own party, the GOP is reacting with increasing indignation. The GOP elders (read heavy donors) want voters to "imagine Donald Trump in the Big Chair in the Oval Office, with responsibilities for worldwide confrontation at his fingertips."

Even though Trump first dabbled in presidential politics as early as the summer of 1987, Trump is not and has never been a career politician. Neither party interests nor a noisy minority defines him or his campaign. Conventional political psychology does not apply when it comes to Trump. Advancement in the GOP, for instances, is not something Trump is betrothed with. Relying on party loyalty, the ability to establish himself as an indispensable expert in a specific policy area, and on finding a mentor that may guide him are, let me put it tactfully, factors probably incompatible with his sense of self. This gives him that rare intestinal fortified that neither his opponents nor our current politicians can afford.

CHAPTER 11

WHAT TO EXPECT IN THE NEXT FOUR YEARS SHOULD TRUMP'S POLITICAL RIVALS BE CORRECT

Well, now that that's over with, where to next?

Truthfully, I'm disappointed the Fed raised interest rates. I expected as much, though I saw reasons why a rate hike would be ill-advised and should have been avoided. There are simply too many deleterious impacts on massively indebted U.S. consumers, American multinational companies slammed by the strengthening dollar and emerging market economies that have taken on trillions in dollar-denominated debt that are getting more and more costly. Those impacts will come home to roost soon enough. Is this the affect of a Trump Presidency? No, but I do believe these presidential events will play a pivotal role in the fluctuation of interest rates over the next few years.

Now, we're supposedly on the march toward three more rate hikes in 2017. Maybe - though doubtful. But we shall see.

1. The stock market certainly got what it thought it wanted, with the DOW reaching it's long-awaited $20,000 mark.

2. Bonds flagged.

3. The dollar rallied.

So many promises/threats are waiting to either unfold or fizzle. Which will Donald Trump show up with in his first year in office?

THE THREAT OF STAGFLATION

Immigrants who make up a solid portion of the service-sector workforce will be supposedly rounded up and summarily dispatched back to their homelands - a massive disruption to restaurant back-of-house operations, the construction industry, agriculture, hotels, landscape companies, etc. This may show a significant brake on economic growth. On the upside, unemployed American citizens will have see more opportunities for employment, should they decide to get their hands dirty and work up a sweat.

Chinese manufacturers/exporters face stiff tariffs as President Trump executes his belief that China is manipulating its currency. That, too, is inflationary and will see China lash out with similar tariffs that hit U.S. exporters, which may lead to layoffs here at home.

U.S. companies also face punitive measures for trying to remain competitive globally by opening production facilities overseas (made all the more important because of the anti-competitive impacts of the strong dollar). This may hit corporate profit margins and lead to declining stock prices and job losses at home.

Meanwhile, infrastructure spending combined with the proposed tax cuts means a fresh round of hell for budget deficits and America's debt. This is stagflationary because the rising cost of government debt payments takes productive capital out of the economy, while infrastructure projects, dump money into the economy which will be chasing goods and services - i.e., rising demand (which will be happening even as all the other inflationary moves unfold).

If the above proves to be true, it poses quite the problem for stocks and bonds, since inflation erodes corporate profits and the value of current bond yields.

A MORE MODERATE APPROACH

As Presidential Trump shows up, we have a slightly brighter path to tomorrow - though economic challenges still exist. Presidential Trump will not provoke a trade war, saving America from another losing battle, while limiting inflationary stresses at home and saving U.S. multinationals from the pain of rapid profit deterioration (nearly half the S&P 500's sales and profits come from overseas).

Nor will Presidential Trump realistically deport 11 million illegal immigrants starting on day one, preventing mass pain across service-sector industries, inside American wallets, and across the broad economy in general.

Nor will he impose punitive measures on American companies that are desperate to remain competitive in a modern global economy. This will preserve corporate profits and limit the impact on stock prices.

Presidential Trump will, however, pursue his infrastructure spending plan, no matter what. This will be inflationary, which means many investors will be adding "hard commodities" to their portfolios - and, in particular, industrial commodities, or "base metals," as they're called, such as copper, nickel, aluminum, and whatnot.

THE WALL

Contrary to popular belief, there is a plan in place by the Trump Administration to have Mexico pay for "the wall". Sure, they may not be directly forking over $10 billion in cash, but the payments are (in theory) going to come indirectly from the Mexican government and its citizens. First, Trump plans to impound all remittance payments. A remittance payment is any money sent from an immigrant in the United States back to their home country. On average, over $20 billion are sent annually from the

United States by illegal immigrants back to their home countries. The idea is that the Mexican government would rather pay half of that to build a wall, as opposed to losing $20 billion a year in GDP.

Secondly, there will be an increase in fees on temporary visas issued to Mexican CEOs and diplomats. In short, the cost for these officials to do business in America will be much higher than it normally has been. There will also be an increase in fees on border crossing cards, not to mention the increase in fees on NAFTA worker visas and ports of entry to the US from Mexico. This is all in addition to the increase on tariffs between the US and Mexico. In theory, these policies are aimed at choking the trade lines between Mexico and the US to the point where Mexico will be asking politely to pay for the wall.

Will the wall actually work? Probably not as much as some might hope; many say that it is more of a "power move" to get the attention of international governments leading towards better trade deals. Would it be the first $10 billion power move made by the US Government? No. Will it be the last? Absolutely not.

CHAPTER 12

MAJOR DIFFERENCES BETWEEN THE REPUBLICANS AND DEMOCRATS

Currently, in the United States, there are two main political parties, the Republican Party and the Democratic Party. While not every person ascribes to every belief of their stated political party, generally, the beliefs held are as follows:

REPUBLICAN PARTY

Republicans prefer a small federal government, only performing those functions that are specifically stated in the Constitution. They believe the federal government should provide for the defense of the country, mint the money and raise the military. They place the freedom and rights of the individual over that of the majority. They believe that taxes should be for the benefit of local government and are opposed to higher taxes. Republicans preserve peace by strengthening the defense. The strength of the nation's economy is in free enterprise and individual and national prosperity. The role of the individual and the family is placed before that of government. Decisions about local matters are made at the local level.

DEMOCRATIC PARTY

Democrats believe the government should be focused at the federal level. They believe the federal government is empowered to do anything that is not specifically prohibited by the Constitution. They believe that the rights of the individual are less important than the good of all. Taxes should be increased and sent to the federal government to disperse for the benefit of the poorest. Democrats believe that money should be spent on social programs rather than defense. They believe world peace can be based on discussion and good intentions. Democrats believe in stronger business regulations and requirements as well as higher taxes. Democrats have been responsible for many of the social programs that place importance on the government's role in caregiving rather than that of the family. Democrats want more federal and state control over the quality and structure of education, particularly at the local level.

Each party believes that they are doing the best for the country. Let no one think that either one or the other is less patriotic. However, good intentions can sometimes still prove to be harmful to a country and its people.

FINAL THOUGHT

All in all, with all political affiliations, biases, and emotions aside, Donald J Trump is the President of the United States of America. I do belive that he has the best intentions for our country, and that he will do everything in his power to make that happen. Do I agree with some of his policies? Yes. Do I disagree with some of them as well? Yes. Am I wishing and hoping for the failure of our President for the sole purpose of proving a point? Absolutely not. To wish failure upon the President of the Unites States is the same as wishing failure upon everyone that lives here. If he or she fails, we fail.

** Thank you very much for sharing an interest in my book. As a writer, I work hard to create and bring accurate, relative content to my readers. If you enjoyed this book, please leave a review on Amazon. If you have any questions, concerns, or criticism, please feel free to email me directly at kconnorsbooks@gmail.com. **